GHOSTS

of the

GARDEN STATE III

LYNDA LEE MACKEN

GHOSTS OF THE GARDEN STATE III

ISBN 0-9755244-1-0

Cover design:
Debra Tremper
Six Penny Graphics, Fredericksburg, VA

Cover photo:
Allentown Feed Company Building

Back cover logo design:
Glenda Moore, catStuff Graphics

Printed on recycled paper by
Sheridan Books, Ann Arbor, MI

All photos by author unless otherwise noted.

CONTENTS

INTRODUCTION

Have you ever had the creepy feeling that something is following you down a dark hallway? Does a chill run up and down your spine when you enter a gloomy basement? If you've answered, "yes" to either or both questions, I'd like to welcome you to the shadow side of the Garden State.

Flip through the pages of *Ghosts of the Garden State III* and enjoy a metaphysical meander through New Jersey's haunted communities.

Learn about historic haunted inns, curious gift shops, and possessed theaters. Gain ghostly entrée to the secrets of an ancient mill and a spirited winery. Hear about extraordinary specters who communicate with the living through electronic voice phenomena (EVP) - spine-tingling evidence of life beyond the grave.

New Jersey's spectral population seems to be growing as rapidly as its human populace. Thanks due in part to high-tech ghost hunters who use state-of-the-art equipment in conducting their research and in their attempts to communicate with the dead.

I admit that my favorite ghost stories are those steeped in history, but readers often ask: "Aren't there any *modern* day ghosts?" Definitely. Check out the hauntings at the Surflight Theater, Liquid Assets Gentlemen's Club, and Rutgers University.

In this third volume of true New Jersey ghost stories, I'd like to update the reader on three eerie locations that initially appeared in the first and second editions of *Ghosts of the Garden State*...

In addition to the ghost boy haunting Clinton's **Red Mill**, psychics detect the spirit of an old, alcoholic gravedigger who accidentally fell off the Clinton **Bridge** and drowned. They sense that his revenant has taken refuge at the museum.

"Phyllis" the **Bernardsville Library** ghost is alive and well, so to speak. In fact, her spirit communicated verbally with paranormal investigator Garrett Husveth in August 2004. This phenomenon was achieved by using a recording device that tape voices below the range of normal hearing.

Husveth set up his electronic equipment throughout the building, that now houses an interior design firm, and asked questions such as: "Is anyone here from the time of the American Revolution?" Phyllis replied in a singsong wail from the former kitchen area: "I'm down in the wall." *Chilling*.

Spirit photographers, Theresa Roguskie and Phyllis Sabia, caught ghostly faces peering out the ancient building's dormer windows.[1]

While visiting the site we all glimpsed the library ghost's spirit in our peripheral vision darting from the structure that for years housed the library, to the newly constructed book depository.

We conducted an impromptu ritual to release Phyllis from her earthbound existence, but a psychic said the library ghost enjoys her earthly abodes - she savors the attention. Phyllis the library ghost has been

---

[1] Unfortunately, the images are too faint to reproduce effectively in black & white, as is the case in some of the stories that follow.

haunting the place for over 250 years - I guess she truly is happy.

A plethora of ghosts haunt Perth Amboy's Proprietary House, one of New Jersey's most haunted historic houses. Psychic Jane Doherty regularly conducts séances for the public in the royal mansion, an activity that greatly perturbs the spirits. (See page 51.)

Since ghosts were once mortal beings the reasons they remain behind are often difficult to fathom. Yet, sometimes it's very clear why, as in the case of an Ocean County resident who shared with me that a ghostly girl inhabited his parents' home.

The Brick towner's aged father was ailing and the specter of a little girl helped the elder get dressed, held his arm to guide him to the bathroom, and assisted him in other ways. The son felt his dad was hallucinating.

After his father passed away, the son stayed in the house with his mother. He awoke one night to see a beautiful young girl standing on the staircase smiling at him. He stressed that she was "the most beautiful little girl" he had ever seen, "a living angel." Indeed she is.

At times, people contact me with suspected hauntings in their homes. The ghostly presences can be disconcerting, and parents fear for their children. Ghosts are rarely harmful - that's only the stuff of movies and television programming intended to scare. The spirits can be counseled that they have died and that it's time for them to move on.

It's time for you to *read* on and get spooked by the unseen world that comes to light on the pages of *Ghosts of the Garden State III* - a paranormal guide to making contact with supernatural New Jersey.

*The Allentown Feed Company building is a converted mill
that houses a restaurant, several shops, and something else...*

ALLENTOWN FEED COMPANY
Allentown

The Allentown Feed Company building, commonly called the Old Mill, was built in 1855 on the foundation of the original "old" mill erected in 1706 by Nathan Allen. Constructed of 300,000 bricks produced on the premises, the gristmill operated on this site for more than 250 years, up until 1963. Today the converted mill houses a restaurant and several shops.

A wall in the former miller's office displays relics of notes and doodles inscribed more than 100 years ago. Spectral vestiges remain as well...

Upon entering the ancient structure I noticed a black figure near the top of the stairs that lead to the basement and heard the tinkling of a tiny bell. Could this shadowy form be the spirit of the man who allegedly fell to his death down the staircase? The chime was definitely *not* the clang of the traditional cowbell that announces diners at the Black Forest Restaurant.

Though subtle, the spectral energy here has workers convinced they share their space with ancient spirits and attribute their eerie feelings to the fallen man's spirit. Especially in the basement feelings of being watched and that they're not alone pervade the place.

A photo taken down below by Theresa Roguskie revealed a traveling sphere of light streaking across the snapshot and another taken upstairs showed more globules. Paranormal investigators contend that "orbs" signify the presence of a life form.

*Psychics assert a Native American spirit resides inside
Eventide Antiques.*

EVENTIDE ANTIQUES
Barnegat

Speaking of bells, shortly after Karen Barchi opened her antique shop in March 2002, she heard bells ring as if to announce a customer coming through the door - yet, no one was there.

No one knows whose spirits reside in the late 19th century commercial building and not only do the invisible ones ring bells, they like to communicate their presence by soft murmurings and ethereal laughter.

Once a co-worker noticed a heavy fireplace poker swaying on its own and a shopper witnessed a startling poltergeist episode when a pottery vase flew off a shelf and streaked across the room.

Another strange event that occurred at Eventide was that when the owner would open the shop, she often found pieces from a vintage, cast-iron Coca Cola® wagon in disarray. She admonished the phantom to tidy up after playing and since then the toys are left in order.

One psychic intuits that the shop's invisible presence is Native American. Unwittingly, Ms. Barchi had envisioned the spirit as a young boy and attributes her perception to her own American Indian ancestry.

As for West Bay Antiques, who shares the building with Eventide, a dealer there said she hears the floors boards creak when no one else is around.

The spirit inside the Surflight Summer Theater is spectacular.

SURFLIGHT THEATER
Beach Haven

In 1950, Joseph P. Hayes, and a cast of 60, breathed life into the Surflight Summer Theatre in an unwieldy 2,200-seat tent.

Six years later, Joe Hayes, donned a clown costume to introduce the Children's Theatre series at the Surflight.

Thanks to Hayes, a former garage soon became the theater's permanent residence and a new costume shop was built next to the playhouse.

But Joe ultimately suffered a fatal heart attack. The theater was shocked and saddened by his untimely passing and in 1980 the Joseph P. Hayes Theatre, Inc. was founded in his memory as a nonprofit organization dedicated to raising scholarship funds.

Theatres are notorious for their spooks and the Surflght is no exception. The scene shop is a room without windows, and despite closed doors, icy breezes turn heads because the chill is usually a prelude to the appearance of a 6-foot-tall indistinct shadow. The form lingers momentarily and then suddenly vanishes.

Workers feel the wraith, whom they've dubbed the "dark man" is the same restless spirit who frequents the catwalk off the Surflight's main stage. Those who encounter the shadowy specter appreciate that this denizen is respectful of the stage and has never disrupted a live performance.

All manner of unexplained events occur in the scene and costume shops - rooms that were originally the old theater. Tools and costumes disappear and turn up days later in weird places.

Several years ago a chalk line, a tool used to make straight lines, went missing. Workers searched all over but couldn't locate the device. They gave up the hunt and went to dinner. Upon their return, there was the gadget sitting in plain sight on top of the tool bucket.

Who is the ghostly culprit? Some think he's an actor who used to work at the Surflight. The performer enjoyed helping out in the costume shop and was a reputed practical jokester.

Most agree, however, that the Surflight is the otherworldly stage for the theater's founder - a volunteer claims that it's Joe Hayes' spirit who lingers in the building. Remarkably, Hayes' ghost once showed up as a "shimmering, translucent" apparition.

Hayes passed away in 1976. One night during that summer, piano music filled the empty Surflight. When the source of the tunes was investigated, there was no (living) body present and *no piano*. In addition to the ghostly melodies, the sound of someone tap dancing on the empty stage also baffled the players.

The finale is that staff members and actors feel comforted that the founder is still looking out for his much-loved showplace.

BELLEVILLE DUTCH REFORMED CHURCH
Belleville

Organized in 1697 as the Second Reformed Church at Second River (today's Passaic River), this Gothic Revival building was erected in 1853. During the Revolutionary War the lofty church steeple housed a Colonial sentry to warn of attacks.

More than any other site in the nation, 67 Revolutionary War veterans are buried in the churchyard, along with members of the Rutgers family.

The Reverend William Moheit, pastor of the 300-year-old church, shepherds a unique parishioner. Musically inclined, the distinctive churchgoer fills the sanctuary with organ music that is literally out of this world because this worshipper is a ghost.

No one knows the identity of the reverent revenant but oftentimes the cleric will hear the church's organist practicing, only to find out that when he enters the church, no one is there.

Supposedly during the War for Independence, militiamen were buried in the basement. Skeletal fragments were unearthed as possible evidence. Could this holy spirit be related to the buried bodies?

Even the customary organist was spooked by the unseen presence. While working on songs for a service all the kneelers started slamming as well as the doors.

Perhaps the phantom organist didn't like anyone else treadling his pedals.

Some say Chester's Publick House bar is a good spot for ghost watching.

PUBLICK HOUSE & HOLLYBERRIES
Chester

Chester's history pre-dates Colonial days. Native American paths along the Black River were trod by the Lenni-Lenape tribe and were the first trails along which white settlers later established farms, mills, and blacksmith shops.

The place where two of these trails or "great roads" crossed was by 1740 known as Black River and by 1771 a weekly stagecoach route extended from Jersey City to the "Crossroads."

In the early 1800's the new and improved Washington Turnpike (now Route 24) ran through what had become known as Chester, and the town was soon home to the "Brick Hotel" built in 1810 by Jacob Drake Jr. and his son, Zephaniah.

During the 19th century, taverns served as town halls hosting meetings where politics were hotly debated. Chester's redbrick Publick House was the central gathering spot in town where people eagerly exchanged news and views.

Jacob Drake's wife disapproved of liquor being served in the tavern because of the establishment's proximity to churches. To add to the historic hotel's mysterious reputation, Mrs. Drake was buried on the property - her earthly remains lay under the parking lot.

In 1867, iron ore was discovered to the north of Main Street and Chester became a boomtown. The iron industry brought railroads and prosperity. Chester enabled Morris County to become the third largest producer of iron ore in the nation by 1880. When the lode was depleted, the boon ended only 25 years after it began. Chester soon became a "ghost town," in more ways than one.

Some assert the Publick House is the most haunted building in Chester, citing the restaurant's bar as a good spot for ghost watching. Apparitions of men in fedoras and women in floor-length ruffled gowns casually drift through the barroom on occasion.

The most popular bedchamber at the Publick House is room 305. According to one bartender, someone died by hanging in that space and ever since occupants sometimes offer a variety of complaints such as the pictures jiggle on the wall, the room gets cold, although the heater is on, and even that the headboard levitates.

A tiny flower-filled park in front of **Hollyberries** belies the fact that the area was once the site of the town's 18th century whipping post.

Could it be that the spirit of someone lynched long ago from the ancient black chestnut tree outside the charming antique shop still hangs around?

The invisible wraith who may reside inside the store manifests in wily ways. The lights in the shop sometimes flicker without anyone touching the switch, merchandise spills from shelves for no reason, and doors close without cause. Spooky!

Could it be that someone lynched from the ancient black chestnut tree outside Hollyberries still hangs around?

Disembodied footsteps heard amid the casks could portend the presence of master vintner Louis Nicholas Renault.

RENAULT WINERY
Egg Harbor City

Louis Nicholas Renault, a master vintner from Rheims, France, arrived in America representing the champagne house of the Duke of Montebello.

A destructive aphid had infiltrated the European vineyards, and the French were desperately looking to save their ravaged vines by grafting to American plants.

Renault first considered California, but results were fruitless so he headed east in 1864 to set down roots.

During the mid 19thcentury, the fertile region between Atlantic City and Philadelphia sprouted with dozens of vineyards; Egg Harbor was celebrated as "wine city."

By 1870, Renault had introduced his New Jersey Champagne and soon he was the largest distributor of sparkling wine in the nation.

Renault Winery is one of our country's oldest, continually operating wineries. A guided tour includes the glass museum, pressing room, where the wines are made, and the aging cellars where an otherworldly but friendly encounter with its founder is a possibility.

Disembodied footsteps heard amid the casks suggest the presence of the master vintner says Charles J. Adams III in *Atlantic County Ghost Stories*. A clanking noise like someone using a wrench is a telltale sign of the winemaker's spirit as is the fleeting face of a gray-bearded man observed peering around corners.

UNION COUNTY COURTHOUSE
Elizabeth

The Union County Courthouse location at Broad Street and Rahway Avenue is steeped in history and lore.

For more than 330 years, a government building has existed on the site. Constructed by early settlers in 1668, a Tory raid destroyed the Elizabethtown Meeting House in 1780. Rebuilt in 1797 and razed again by fire in 1808, the edifice was replaced in 1810; the present day 1905 courthouse, celebrates its centennial this year.

The courthouse stands adjacent to the historic First Presbyterian Church where many notable citizens are interred including Hannah Caldwell[2] and her husband James, known as the "Fighting Parson." Hannah was shot and killed in front of her children at her home.

It is unclear whether the parson's wife was slain by a stray bullet as she worked in her kitchen or, as the populace believed, murdered by a British soldier. Regardless, her death became a battle cry for the mercenaries who assembled in unprecedented numbers to oppose the enemy.

It was Hannah's death that inspired the Union County Seal dedicated to the fallen patriot.

In the past, some night crew workers proclaimed that Hannah's diaphanous ghost floated down the halls and eerily strolled the churchyard's burial ground.

---

[2] A portrait of Hannah hangs in an upstairs room of the church.

OUR HOUSE RESTAURANT
Farmingdale

The landmark restaurant at 420 Adelphia Road predates the American Revolution. Built in 1747, by George Marriner, it operated for a long time as "Marriner's Tavern," then later as "Our House Tavern."

For many years the restaurant served as a gathering place for a band of outlaws known as the "Fagen Gang." A bit of macabre history is that members of Major Lee's Light Dragoons hanged Lewis Fenton, one of the gang members, on September 23, 1779 in front of the tavern.

Our House Restaurant is the second-oldest restaurant in Monmouth County; when all is quiet at the historic eatery, unusual things occur.

During a 1998 renovation, new owner Jeff Wish noticed ceiling fans and lights turned on by themselves. Another night as he put money away in an upstairs safe, the door to a small room, always tightly secured, opened and a strange noise issued from within. Wish didn't stick around to investigate - he bolted down the stairs.

Since that time, no one stays alone in the restaurant. There's disembodied footsteps heard overhead in the empty rooms, the kitchen door creaks even though it's not moving, and the pictures that decorate the walls suddenly shift askew.

Is the hanged hooligan the culprit? Who knows. But rest assured that whoever haunts the restaurant is a benevolent spirit.

A bit of macabre history is that one of Fagen's gang members was hanged in front of the Our House Restaurant.

*Country Sisters, 110 South Main Street, Forked River
is home to a ghost.*

COUNTRY SISTERS & RITE-AID DRUGS
Forked River

The house that's home to the Country Sisters Gift Shop was the mortal abode of Mrs. Aspinwall, wife of a Methodist minister. The elderly lady died while trying on a hat when she was 103 years old.

Ms. Aspinwall's claim to fame was that she once shook Abraham Lincoln's hand. Local boys often knocked on her door to ask for the privilege of shaking the hand that had grasped Lincoln's.

Obviously reluctant to give up the ghost while alive, her outlook remains the same in death.

The three sisters who own the property say they occasionally hear the woman's spirit sighing in the store and hear her footsteps upstairs.

Since the aged woman loved opera music, the owners used to leave the radio on when they closed up shop. Left tuned to either a popular or country station, when they returned in the morning, a classical station would be playing.

Just a few doors south on Route 9 is a Rite-Aid Drug Store where another female ghost is on display.

In the beginning of the 19th century as the lumber and bog ore industries declined, fishing, oystering, and the pleasure resort trade became major industries in sparsely populated Lacey Township.

The Parker House became an important stagecoach stop and was one of a number of large hotels in town. Built by Sheriff Parker and his son in the 1880s, the hostelry was purchased in 1911, by Frank Briggs who renamed the establishment the Greyhound Inn.

Today's Rite-Aid stands on the site and couldn't look less spooky, yet the staff claims the place is inhabited by a watchful presence.

One night after closing, an employee noticed that the items she had just shelved were rearranged - yet no one else was in the store. Another worker claimed she couldn't get the supply door closed because someone unseen defied her efforts. After hours, two employees heard someone sashaying about the center aisle.

The most astonishing incident in the store was the appearance of Josephine Parker Applegate's ghost.

Josephine was Sheriff Parker's daughter and married Howard Applegate in 1895. The couple managed the hotel together but Josephine's talent was in the kitchen - her meals were legendary along the Jersey Shore.

Mahala Landrum is Frank Briggs daughter and she lived at the Greyhound Inn. She wrote in *The Forked River Gazette*, that as a child, her mother described Josephine as tall with brown hair; she had a nervous twitch that could be relieved by stroking people's ears.

Ms. Landrum related that when she was about ten years old, one of the inn's guests was shocked to see the apparition of a tall brunette bending over his bed. The spirit spoke to him from the foot of the bed.

When Mahala was a teenager, her aunt had an unforgettable encounter with the sheriff's daughter's specter. The woman awoke with a start when she felt someone rubbing her ear and witnessed Josephine's ghost at her bedside.

Rowan University admits several ghosts.

ROWAN UNIVERSITY
Glassboro

For years rumors swirled that Tohill Auditorium was haunted by it's namesake, Elizabeth Tohill. Students, faculty, and employees reported strange events occurring inside the building.

According to *Haunted New Jersey* (Martinelli & Stansfield), Tohill was a drama teacher at the school from 1930-1956. Her apparition appears backstage and showed up in a video of a chorus line as an extra dancer.

Apparitions, baffling noises and doors opening on their own are some other anomalies described by witnesses. Sensing a presence not of this world, ghost busters were summoned - the South Jersey Ghost Research Team.

Without a doubt, the group's investigations obtained convincing results. Motion sensors detected stirring in the back of the auditorium when the entire team, led by Dave Juliano, was on the stage. A moment later, the group observed a male apparition walk toward the auditorium's rear entrance.

As investigators tested the site, they all experienced a variety of sensations. Although never threatening, "something" brushed against them and touched their hair, head, and face. They experienced dizziness, ears popping, tingling, nausea, and a heavy, "foggy" feeling.

One team member received a clear impression of a woman wearing an old-fashioned, white dress, and her hair coiffed in a bun.

They obtained positive electromagnetic field (EMF) readings on their meters and dozens of light orbs appeared in their photos.

Footsteps were heard on the stage, and a tall dark shadow ambled stage left. A psychic member intuited the image of a young man in his late teens or early twenties, with dark slicked-back hair, dressed in a white t-shirt and jeans. She perceived that he had fallen onto the stage while building a set. The icy chill that coursed up her spine enforced her perception.

When investigators noticed movements in their peripheral vision they saw their equipment flash abnormally and the fresh batteries in their cameras went dead as they discerned a presence in their midst. (Spirits draw energy from power sources in order to manifest.)

Another oddity was that the atmosphere felt as if the temperature plummeted yet no temperature change registered on their gauges.

Throughout their investigation numerous shadows and movements were perceived throughout the entire auditorium. The sight of phantom heads bobbing up and down in the seating area was downright unnerving.

Scientists speculate that some structures can trap the vibrations of sounds, and even emotions, and store them indefinitely due to the building's construction materials. Matters such as quartz crystals, silica, and ferric salts are the same substances used in manufacturing some recording equipment.

This theory could account for the hauntings occurring at Rowan's Tohill Auditorium - leftover energies replaying mortal events over and over like a never-ending audio/video tape.

Is the Batsto mansion really haunted or is it just the imagination of tourists?

BATSTO MANSION
Hammonton

The Batsto Village Restoration and nearby Atsion Lake located in Wharton State Forest offers a glimpse of life in the Pine Barrens from the 1760s to the 1850s. The historic site's centerpiece is the Richards-Wharton Mansion.

Charles Read is credited with building the Batsto Iron Works along the Batsto River in 1766. The area offered the natural resources necessary for making iron. Bog ore was mined from the banks of streams and rivers, trees fueled the fires, and water powered the manufacturing.

The Iron Works produced household wares such as cooking pots and kettles. During the Revolutionary War, Batsto manufactured supplies for the Continental Army.

In 1784, William Richards managed the industry and erected the 32-room mansion. The residence served generations of ironmasters and reflects the prosperity enjoyed during Batsto's heyday.

By the mid 1800's, iron production declined and Batsto became a glassmaking community known for its windowpanes.

Joseph Wharton, a Philadelphia businessman, purchased Batsto in 1876. Wharton continued to purchase property in the surrounding area and improved many village buildings. His renovation of the ironmaster's mansion transformed the structure into the elegant Italianate manse we know today.

Fourteen rooms, including the parlors, dining room, library and bedrooms, are currently open to the public.

Some visitors claim the place is haunted according to Charles Adams III in his book *Ghosts of Atlantic County*. He states that tourists have observed a figure peering out the upper floor windows. Some have even captured the human likeness in their photos.

During the 1930s and 40s, Elizabeth Brown Pezzuto's aunt and uncle were caretakers at the mansion. Elizabeth recalls that when her uncle trudged up the winding staircase carrying an oil lamp to light his way, the lantern cast flickering shadows. The eerie images on the walls gave her goose bumps.

It might be that pranks played by Elizabeth and her sisters precipitated the mansion's haunted reputation.

When the girls heard people walking about the grounds, they would watch as the visitors approached the house to peek in the windows, just as sightseers do today. That's when the sisters reveled in pretending the mansion was haunted.

The girls would grab pillows from the sofa and chairs and hide under the windowsills. Then, when they heard the people's comments as they gazed through the windows, the girls would toss the pillows up in the air giving the peeping toms a good scare!

Technology is helping us get closer to confirming the existence of ghosts, but in order to establish this place as haunted, proof is elusive and remains up in the air, just like the pillows once tossed by mischievous little girls.

THE BRASS RAIL RESTAURANT
Hoboken

The Brass Rail Restaurant was the setting of a celebration turned tragic when a young bride accidentally fell to her death on her wedding day. Since then her invisible presence has created quite a stir inside the elegant restaurant.

Hauntings are a rarity but they can occur at the place of an unexpected and traumatic event. Due to the suddenness of the passing, the entity is confused and doesn't realize they're dead. Probably this is the case at the Brass Rail.

Employees have felt a disembodied shove as they make their way down the scene of the accident - the curving staircase that leads from the balcony.

The incorporeal bride tries to use the phone to communicate. Several times the telephone lights up announcing an incoming call, yet it doesn't ring. When answered, no one is there.

Another haunting theory is that past events are somehow imprinted on the structure, like voices on audiotape or images on videotape, and can play over and over.

In this instance, that could explain the sounds of guests enjoying a festive party heard when the restaurant is empty.

THE HERMITAGE
Ho Ho Kus

Mary Elizabeth Rosencrantz was born in the Hermitage and lived there until she died in 1970 at the age of 85.[3] Unmarried and one of the last descendants of Elijah Rosencrantz who purchased the Hermitage in 1807, she knew the historical value of her home and willed it to the State of New Jersey for use as a museum and park.[4]

In order to preserve the historic property for posterity, Mary Elizabeth and Katie Zahner, a former servant, endured many years of hardship. They couldn't afford to heat the entire house so they resided in two rooms relying on a woodstove for warmth and cooking. The Red Cross brought them food, and they received coal from railroad workers. The pair warded off trespassers and vandals. Only when the women took ill did social service install in one room the home's first electricity in 1969.[5]

Mary Elizabeth routinely refused offers to purchase the 5-acre manor even though selling meant comfort for the aging women. Rosencrantz's determination to save her beloved property was unyielding.

The distinctive stone estate predates the American Revolution and the Gothic structure hosted a long list of notables including George Washington, James Monroe,

---

[3] Her faithful companion, Katie Zahner, died five days later.
[4]Text cited from on-site historical marker.
[5] www.hermitage.org.

... the flickering glow traveled from room to room as if Mary Elizabeth's indomitable spirit performed a post-mortem vigil.

Aaron Burr, Marquis de Lafayette, Alexander Hamilton, Benedict Arnold and his wife-to-be, Peggy Shippen, to name just a few.

The home's spectacular guest register is impressive but the most intriguing visitor of all may be the ghost that is said to haunt this noteworthy house, even though dedicated staffers cannot confirm or deny the existence of a supernatural presence at the site.

After Mary Elizabeth passed away, the Hermitage fell into disrepair. The grounds grew dark and ominous and the house slowly decayed.

Those who dared to trespass got goose bumps when they heard the sound of faint piano music coming from inside the forsaken structure. Some locals who passed by the house often claimed to see a light inside. Barely discernable, the flickering glow traveled from room to room as if Mary Elizabeth's indomitable spirit performed a post-mortem vigil, roaming the manse with a candle to watch over the space.

Another intriguing Hermitage mystery is the "secret room." The unremarkable storage space turned spectacular in tantalizing stories recounted by Mary Elizabeth and her Aunt Bess when they ran their popular Tea Room in the 1920s.

One tale told of the discovery of a human skeleton inside the small space dressed in the disintegrating remains of a Hessian uniform but draped with an American flag.

*This remarkable photo taken on Spruce Road in Howell
Township by Trish Hruska may be evidence of a supernatural
presence. Legend says a little girl, who has come to be known
as "Ann Marie," wandered into the Howell woods and never
came out. At times, unexplainable screaming noises emanate
from the woods in the early evening hours. Some say they've
heard a disembodied, distressed voice crying out for help.*

34

PRIVATE RESIDENCE
Howell

On Halloween Night 2002, Trish Hruska of Howell Township, snapped a photo of her neighbor's porch with a digital camera, but what developed instead was astonishing.

After giving it some thought, her neighbor, Barbara Mocarski, was not surprised because encounters with the paranormal have been the norm since she moved to her house on Pine Road.

Barbara writes: *"When I first moved in I heard a baby crying. My husband thought I was hearing things until one day he was standing in the living room with me and heard it too. Another time we were in our bedroom with the door closed and heard a knock on the door. No one was home - our children were at their friends' house and our front door was locked. Lights in the bedroom keep going on in the middle of the night and footsteps resound near the door."*

Barbara's daughter Lisa saw a colorful round light enter her bedroom, circle a stuffed animal, and then disappear. Once when Lisa was walking down the street with a friend they felt someone watching them; looking back they witnessed a young girl dressed in white. When they looked again, the girl was gone.

Most extraordinary was when Barbara's husband observed a male figure standing in the hall. He waited a long time to share his experience so as not to scare his family. *Ghosts are everywhere...*

Virginia Tavern
Jersey City

One day while Frank Couzze was alone in his tavern, he heard an ethereal female voice call his name. He has owned the bar located at the corner of Virginia and Mallory Avenues for 25 years and always had the feeling that something was "not quite right" with the place.

Workers catch sight of furtive figures in their peripheral vision and sometimes when bar patrons turn to talk to an adjacent customer, there's no one there.

When a regular mentioned that she felt someone tap her shoulder, Frank's suspected that his watering hole was haunted.

In addition to spectral touching, others report beer cans fly off shelves, unpleasant odors linger, and cold spots cause shivers. First and foremost is that every now and then, a friendly, young female apparition shows up.

Tri-State Paranormal Research taped an eerie, voice whispering the name "Luke Tanner." The New Jersey-based group's photos revealed orbs of light and their equipment measured unusual temperature fluctuations - all evidence that "something" was trying to manifest.

Several people, who either owned or resided at the property, died in recent years, yet "no conclusive evidence exists that the spirits of any of these individuals remain with the property."[6]

---

[6] www.tsprghosts.com

TENNENT CHURCH
Manalapan

This story is more *haunting* than it is haunted.

On Sunday morning, June 28, 1778, General George Washington and about six thousand men, hastily passed by Old Tennent on their way from Englishtown where the sound of cannons alerted them to a battle with the British. By evening the enemy was driven back - a much needed and hard won victory of one of the longest battles of the Revolution.

The Tennent Church served as a hospital after the Battle of Monmouth.

At the height of the hostilities, embattled soldiers were carried to the church where members of the congregation tended to their needs. As the injured lay suffering, musket balls bombarded the vulnerable refuge - some blasts managed to breach the walls.

One exhausted American combatant tried to make his way to the building but had to stop and rest for a moment on Sarah Mattison's grave. As he sat in a war-induced daze, the soldier was struck by a cannon ball that blasted off a piece of Sarah's headstone.

Onlookers hurried him into the church where he was laid out on one of the pews. His bloodstains *are still visible* beneath the cushion of the second pew from the back of the historic church. For a while, the soldier's bloody handprint mark was also visible on the pew's book rest up until the wood was grained.

Tennent Church's peaceful setting obscures its place in our nation's early struggle.

WENONAH CEMETERY
Mantua

Legend says "Wenonah" is the name of a beautiful Sioux maiden who killed herself rather than marry a man she did not love. But is the mythical woman the cause of the bloodcurdling screams that emanate from the graveyard at night and plague locals?

On several occasions law enforcement investigated the shrieking by searching among the tombstones with dogs, high-powered searchlights, and a thermal-imaging camera that detects body heat. A helicopter from the Camden County Sheriff's Office scanned the cemetery with a high-tech camera - but to no avail.

The source of the ungodly noise remains a mystery and provokes the theory that the cemetery is haunted.

Dave Juliano, director of South Jersey Ghost Research, frequently visits Wenonah Cemetery where paranormal activity is so frequent that he utilizes the site as a training ground for novice investigators.

Juliano's group uses special cameras and an array of devices to record temperature changes and electro-magnetic-field (EMF) variations as a means to justify the unexplained. Ghostly orbs appear in photographs, certain trees trigger aberrant EMF readings, and mausoleums register extreme temperature changes.

Once, Juliano himself saw an indistinct male silhouette jog past the life-size statue of Marine lieutenant, George B. Batten (1890 - 1926).

RUTGERS UNIVERSITY
New Brunswick

Rutgers University was founded in 1766 as Old Queens College. According to college folklore, a sad specter, dressed in old lace and known as the "Gray Lady," is only one of the spirits who haunt the historic campus.

Shortly after the Revolutionary War, Alexander Hamilton became infatuated with Catherine Livingston, the daughter of General William Livingston, the first governor of New Jersey and namesake of Livingston College. The ill-fated couple faced disparity in their social standing so the courtship proved futile.

Female ghosts who suffered an unrequited love are often referred to as "gray ladies." Could the lady in gray that roams the olden campus be Catherine Livingston still pining away for Alexander?

Over sixty years ago, Mabel Smith Douglass, founder of Rutgers University's Douglass College, drowned in Lake Placid, New York. Her diaphanous spirit sometimes hovers over the lake where she died and her residual energy may be the cause of some pretty strange happenings at her beloved campus.

Mabel Smith Douglass was born in Jersey City to a successful merchant and she married an equally prosperous businessman. Enough for most women of her generation, Douglass had greater ambitions.

One of the first graduates of Barnard College, she realized the importance of education and endeavored tirelessly to found a woman's college in New Jersey as a companion college to Rutgers.

In 1916, her husband died after only thirteen years of marriage and she was left to raise two small children and run the family business. Despite these new challenges, Douglass' realized her vision two years later, with the establishment of the New Jersey College for Women; she was named its first dean.

Her career flourished for five years and she became a legendary figure at the school, devoting countless hours to her vocation and the students' welfare. She labored late into the night and slept on a cot at the school.

On September 9, 1923 tragedy struck when her son died in their home at 135 George Street, today's Douglass Writing Center. William reportedly shot himself in the house.

Numerous achievements followed the terrible loss. Douglass received an honorary doctorate of laws, beautiful Voorhees Chapel opened on campus, and she was appointed to the New Jersey State Board of Education. In 1930, Douglass became the first woman to receive Columbia University's medal for distinguished public service. Russell Sage College presented her with an honorary doctorate degree and she was named *Officier d'Academie* by the French government for promoting French language education in America.

After all this, Douglass suffered a nervous breakdown and voluntarily committed herself to a private mental hospital in Westchester County, New York for a year.

Upon her release, she resigned her position as dean and retreated to her Camp Onondaga on Lake Placid.

On the last day of her stay at her Adirondack refuge Douglass set off to supposedly pick some autumn leaves. But instead she rowed across Lake Placid to Pulpit Rock where the water's depth is reportedly fathomless.

Years later, two workmen publicly declared that they saw Douglass out on the lake standing in her skiff with a veil over her head. They then claimed she threw something into the water and she followed in after it overturning the boat in the process. The men rushed to the spot, and righted the boat only to find the oars neatly tucked under the seats and, unfortunately, no trace of the woman.[7]

Douglass' death was officially ruled an accident.

Thirty years later, on September 15, 1963, *almost to the day*, two divers discovered her body sixty feet from Pulpit Rock. At first they thought the figure was a mannequin, but when they grabbed the arm and the limb released from the body, they knew then they had found a corpse.

Due to the frigid temperature and natural chemicals in the water, Douglass' fatty tissues virtually turned to wax, a process called saponification.

Since Douglass had no living relatives, Rutgers claimed the body and her remains were interred in the family plot next to her husband and her son.

Strangely enough, Douglass' daughter Edith also suffered the death of her husband at an early age; she eventually committed suicide.

---

[7] George C. Ortloff, A *Lady in the Lake*, 1985.

In 1955, the NJ College for Women was officially renamed Douglass College in honor of Mabel Smith Douglass and her accomplishments in founding and firmly establishing the college.

Some students speculate that Douglass, or her children, are responsible for the supposed haunting of the Little Theater on the Douglass Campus.

The Little Theater was the first theater and drama building on the college grounds. According to hearsay, students witnessed the spirit of an older woman playing the theater's piano and some heard her singing.

When Jane Inge, faculty member and director of productions for the building, did not approve of the way rehearsals were going she flickered the lights. Now, lights flicker during bad rehearsals - as done by her personage in life. Perhaps the ghost is Ms. Inge, not Mabel at all.

Yet another strong-willed university woman is the wraith of Mary Putnam Woodbury Neilson.

Primarily recognized for her exquisite roses, Douglass' Woodbury and Bunting-Cobb residence hall was built over Neilson's rose gardens. Students feel her restless spirit inhabits the campus evidenced by roses that die overnight when placed anywhere on the first floor of the Woodbury section of the hall.

Rutgers' student newspaper, *The Daily Targum*, periodically recounts the spooky oft-told legends of two College Avenue statues. James Suydam's effigy haunts students by appearing to watch their every move and the statue of Prince William the Orange on the Voorhees Mall, also known as "Silent Willy," is supposed to whistle at virgin girls as they pass.

HOLY CROSS CEMETERY
North Arlington

Vanishing hitchhiker stories are legendary and flourish in just about every state. Here's one of New Jersey's versions...

Over 50 years ago, a couple was out for a drive along Belleville Turnpike in North Arlington. They were about a quarter of a mile away from the light that currently stands at Schuyler Avenue.

The pair noticed a young girl standing on the side of the road. The 7 or 8 year old was wearing her First Holy Communion dress and appeared as an angelic vision. The youngster stood perfectly still while holding a small bunch of flowers and prayer book in her hands.

Concerned that the girl was all alone, the couple offered her a ride home. The little girl climbed into their vehicle and gave the driver an address on Ridge Road.

When the twosome arrived at the stated address, they were taken aback for they were at the front gate of Holy Cross Cemetery.

As they turned around in unison to tell the girl that she must have been mistaken, the little communicant was gone - yet her tiny bouquet remained behind laying on the back seat.

Although the lighthouse itself is not haunted, the spirit of a former keeper still struggles in the inlet tides.

HEREFORD INLET
North Wildwood

Late in the 19th century, in the then known fishing village of Anglesea, a much needed lifesaving station was constructed to serve the growing number of mariners navigating the perilous Atlantic Coastline with its shifting sand bars and treacherous currents. The lighthouse was erected shortly thereafter in 1871.

Today's Hereford Inlet Lighthouse is listed in the National Registry of Historic Places. The Victorian era dwelling is the only example of Swiss Gothic architecture on the East Coast and features five fireplaces; the beacon resembles a comfortable home more than it does a traditional lighthouse. Without a doubt, many vied for the coveted lighthouse keeper position at this location.

Open for public tours during the summer, visitors may stroll about the spectacular flower and herb gardens reminiscent of those cultivated a century ago. They may even glimpse the specter of a former lighthouse tender that drowned in the turbulent inlet waters while attempting a rescue.

Although the lighthouse itself is not haunted, those who've witnessed the keeper's unsettled specter claim his disturbed spirit still struggles in the stormy seas.

ALFRED T. RINGLING MANOR
Oak Ridge

Over 100 years ago, Alfred T. Ringling originally created the circus as entertainment for his son. Ringling eventually took his show on the road and the rest is history.

The ringmaster purchased Petersburg Pond and 1,000 well-secluded acres off Oak Ridge Road in Jefferson Township as a winter sanctuary.

Between 1913 and 1916 the construction of Ringling's manor ensued and ultimately boasted 28 rooms, a colossal pipe organ, Tiffany windows, and a massive hand carved fireplaces. A boathouse, garage, blacksmith shop, water tower, and large animal barns were built. The showman housed elephants, giraffes, lions, tigers, and bears on the estate.

In the 1950's, the Catholic Church purchased the property for use as a monastery.

As it turns out, the spirits of the long gone circus animals haunt the property - their spectral roars and cries trapped in time. Locals shared that when they were kids they perceived an assortment of animal sounds emanate from the old empty cages.

The friars offered nothing unusual but admitted the old manor produces creepy, creaky noises on occasion.

Could the spirit of Daisy the Elephant be prowling about the ethers, or are her phantom bellows just a figment of a child's imagination?

During the renovation of Somewhere Inn Time, a spectral burglar paid a visit and the chandelier mysteriously swayed.

SOMEWHERE INN TIME
Ocean City

When Scott and Nancy Robel first moved into their 1896 Queen Anne Victorian they often heard disembodied footsteps, yet when they investigated the sounds, no one was ever found.

The numerous inexplicable events that transpired during the renovation of the house astonished the couple.

Robel repeatedly heard what sounded like an interloper climbing through a third-floor window from the fire escape and depositing tools on the hardwood floor. Certain they had a burglar in the house, Scott approached the area with caution yet didn't find anyone trespassing.

Nancy stared in awe as the parlor chandelier wobbled without cause - a disturbing and frightful spectacle.

When representatives from South Jersey Paranormal Research investigated the property with video and digital cameras, audio equipment, electromagnetic field detectors and other gadgets utilized to hunt ghosts, they felt there was "a lot going on."

Bottom line is that the bed & breakfast inn is full of love and the Robels consider their amiable, invisible guests pleasant company.

PATERSON CITY HALL
Paterson

Paterson is long on history and that is likely what makes the metropolis so haunted.

The decorative City Hall building is one of many spirited sites and remains the otherworldly stomping ground of its former mayor Frank X. Graves Jr. His disembodied footsteps echo through the building when the daily bustle dies down and his honor can stroll alone.

According to psychic medium Jane Doherty, Graves hangs around because he's unhappy that the mayor's office was moved from the public safety building to City Hall after he died in 1990.

Doherty contacts spirits in a very unique way. When she encounters a wayward soul, her stomach slowly expands. Then she closes her eyes and envisions an image of what's going on. That's how she divines the identity of the spirit(s) and the reason(s) they remain behind.

Doherty conducts ghost tours of Paterson as well. At the Main Street Square Mall the psychic's burgeoning stomach clued her in on the otherworldly presence of a firefighter who perished in a 1991 blaze that destroyed the Meyer Brothers Department Store once occupying the site.

Doherty also intuits native son Lou Costello's spirit dwelling inside the city's museum.

PROPRIETARY HOUSE
Perth Amboy

At a Proprietary House séance conducted by Jane Doherty, the psychic stated that one of the "house spirits" wanted to "pinch my butt!" Don Peck thought the playful soul might be "Harold," an on-site caretaker who died holding a drink in his hand. He stated that on occasion the scent of alcohol permeates the old dwelling.

As President Emeritus of the Proprietary House Association, Don Peck is in the position to know well of the spectral shenanigans at the country's only remaining royal governor's house erected in 1764 for His Excellency William Franklin, Governor of the Province of New Jersey - and Benjamin Franklin's son.

In 1775, the elder Franklin journeyed to Perth Amboy to persuade his son to withdraw his allegiance from Britain. The senior statesman pleaded, ranted, and raved, but William would not be swayed. Benjamin grieved over his failure to convert William, and later wrote to a friend, "I am deserted by my only son."

Governor Franklin was arrested in 1776 for supporting the British.

Peck shared that the sound of heavy footsteps is often heard inside the house. Incredibly the thud of purposeful strides was audible overhead during the séance. Could the pensive pacing be William's spirit mulling over his options?

The Proprietary House is one of New Jersey's most haunted historic houses.

After the Revolution, the interior of the governor's house was destroyed by fire, but later restored, enlarged, and established as the Brighton House. For a few years, the hotel, which catered to the rich and fashionable, flourished but business dwindled during the War of 1812.

In the atmospheric wine cellar that functions as a tearoom, Peck said a visitor once observed a spectral Revolutionary War soldier walk right *through* the brick wall. Oftentimes it appears that invisible guests are enjoying an otherworldly tea break. Volunteers find two chairs pulled out from the table, as if occupied by patrons, and two cups righted on the saucers when normally the cups are set upside down.

Sometimes during a formal tea, the embarrassing stench of horse manure filters through from another dimension. In truth, animals were kept in the house to secret them from marauding adversaries.

The ladies room is another site where a mischievous spirit likes to play with the toilet tissue and detains occupants by locking the door. (I couldn't enter the dark restroom until someone turned on the light - but then again, I'm a scaredy cat!).

Locals assert the place remains haunted by the specter of a little boy dressed in blue antique garb. (Is he a revenant from the Brighton House?). Neighbors say they see him knocking at the front door and even tell of the ghost boy playing in their yards.

The former carriage house is nearby and the older couple who resides there claims that now and again an ethereal Victorian couple appears in their bedroom.

Without question, old Perth Town's royal palace continues to intrigue historians *and* ghost hunters alike.

The wait staff contends that three different spirits haunt the West Side Tavern.

THE WEST SIDE TAVERN
Point Pleasant

The West Side Tavern patrons enjoy dining with spirits - in more ways than one.

Three ghosts supposedly haunt the 19th century building, one being the disturbed spirit of "Captain John" who resides in the attic and is known to stomp about the second floor.

Legend says that the hateful captain abused his teenage daughter Elsie, (she could have been his niece), and the girl hid in the closet to escape his cruelty. Her bedroom remains intact and many workers refuse to even go near her closet claiming they hear noises emanating from the storage space. Could the sounds be psychic debris of the terror recorded on the premises so long ago?

A newspaper photographer found it impossible to snap shots in the room - his camera refused to focus.

Patrons and workers claim to hear footsteps running through the forsaken region of the second floor. Is this the evil captain still chasing after Elsie?

The final ghost residing in the casual eatery is a young boy who hangs out in the main dining area and enjoys karaoke. People allege to have heard him sing along to songs and make accompanying noises not normally a part of the music.

The phantom boy tickles the ivories every now and then and even tosses the speakers if he gets angry. He is blamed for another audio oddity as well. Sometimes the jukebox will often repeat the 13th song selection.

Waitresses, bartenders and patrons have witnessed dishes smashing, spooky silhouettes, and Captain John's full-bodied apparition. Boxes fly, lights flicker, and a former employee recalled the basement door mysteriously slammed behind her one night.

The haunted eatery was featured on *The Jenny Jones Show* and avid ghost hunters often visit.

The building, which dates to 1870, served as a hotel, brothel, and temporary morgue for victims of the *John Minturn* shipwreck on February 15, 1846, which killed 39 people. The tavern operated as a stagecoach stop at the time of the disaster.

Tavern owners Jack Vitale and Jenna Canale view the tales of ghosts and hauntings with a grain of salt although Canale greets the ghosts when opening and closing the bar.

Shortly after they purchased the tavern, Vitale removed some furniture from the attic, including a broken chair that sat in a shadowy corner. His cousin visited a psychic who said the spirit wants their chair back. The psychic had no prior knowledge of the incident and Vitale swiftly returned the chair to its place.

When ghost hunters investigated the upper floor with digital cameras, audio equipment and electromagnetic testing devices, they found evidence of a spectral presence only in the corner where the chair sits. Orbs of light were visible in photos taken in that area of the attic as well.

SUNNYBANK
Pompton Lakes

The grounds of Terhune Memorial Park pulsate with a "magic charm." Even though Terhune and his frolicking collies are long gone, the property is still a paradise thanks to Wayne Township's Department of Parks & Recreation who own and maintain the acreage.

Originally a parcel of the Arent Schuyler crown grant of 1695, the property provides a direct link with New Jersey's American Revolutionary past. During the harsh winter of 1777-78, the Van Cortlandt Regiment encamped in the Sunnybank meadow.

Reverend Edward Payson Terhune, who purchased the land in the late 1860s, found the remains of an American officer who was buried with a British trophy sword. His son, Albert, found Hessian handcuffs and corroded cannonballs while hiking the Ramapo hills.

Lad, and all those collies that were the subject of Terhune's books, lived out their days at Sunnybank and are buried on the property - some in their favorite shady spots when alive. On June 28, 1923, "Wolf's" obituary appeared nationally in newspapers; the brave collie died on the railroad tracks in Pompton Lakes attempting to save a mongrel.

Rex qualifies as Sunnybank's ghost. Visitors witnessed this mighty collie-mix, unaware the dog was dead. The dog's apparition often sat next to Terhune as he napped in his favorite chair.

RARITAN LIBRARY
Raritan

At odd hours of the night, neighbors see lights go on and off in this 18th century building. They report frequent sightings of an elderly woman in certain windows and in the garden behind the building.

The Raritan Public Library is housed in the former home of General John Frelinghuysen - patriarch of one of the most prominent families of New Jersey.

The property was originally part of a large tract of land purchased by Dutch settlers in 1683 from Native Americans for a mere pittance.

Built in the early 1700s, the west wing, now the library's "children's room," is the oldest section of the house and functioned as a tavern, as well as a public meeting hall and jail.

The small wooden structure bordered the Old York Road, the one time wilderness trail that grew into a major thoroughfare connecting New York and Philadelphia. The residence also served as a welcomed respite on the Underground Railroad.

In 1971, the historic house was placed on the National Register and New Jersey Register of Historic Places. A partial restoration and additions readied the building for use as a library.

In the morning, opening staffers sporadically hear someone walking around. They pay no attention because they think it's just another employee until they realize they're all alone - or are they?

Another phenomenon is the aroma of old-fashioned aftershave and pipe tobacco that pervades the tranquil atmosphere. The sound of doors opening and closing is unexplainable as are the attic windows that refuse to stay closed on occasion.

Librarian Jackie Widows shared that once a terrified teenaged girl came flying down the stairs because she said she heard the sound of ghostly laughter. The girl raced out the front door in a panic.

One more story Ms. Widows offered was that of an agitated young mother who was clearly upset over her toddler's screaming because the child was afraid of "the man standing over there," except no one *but* the child witnessed the man.

The janitor told his tale of hearing people talking downstairs when he was in the building after hours alone. On occasion, even staff members hear the mysterious voices as they descend the stairs.

During a 1995 renovation the door slammed shut in a room where the painter was working. When the worker went to exit he could not get out and felt an invisible someone held the door closed in order to keep him trapped. Upon his release he walked out the library and never went back.

A carpenter, and even certain patrons, refuse to set foot in the building ever again, and they decline to discuss their reasons why.

So when books pop off shelves and fall to the floor, it may be an earlier tenant trying to make you remember a morsel of the history that has gone before.

OLD STONE HOUSE
Sewell

When Cookie Kaizar, and a small army of volunteers, began the awesome task of restoring Washington Township's Old Stone House she felt "guided" by an unseen presence and even received inspiration through her dreams.

Spirits will use any available energy source to manifest their presence and at the Open House celebration for the 1730 structure the invisible inhabitant flickered the candle flames erratically to show its appreciation.

On another occasion, when Cookie was alone in the house she noticed the candle flame wavering wildly. She grew sensitive to the spirit's method of communication and knew this was a signal. Sure enough there was a knock at the door - the presence warned her there was someone coming up the back path. Cookie felt certain she and the house were protected by the indiscernible specter.

On the other hand, others believed they were targeted for teasing and when they felt unseen fingers tousling their hair, they ran screaming from the house.

While weeding the herb garden, Cookie heard three taps on the window yet no one was in the house. The three taps continued until finally she noticed a middle-aged female apparition, with no discernable facial features, peering out an upstairs window.

Liquid Assets Gentlemen's Club
South Plainfield

When strange, glowing objects materialized on Liquid Assets' surveillance cameras positioned both inside and out, one disc jockey decided to "stake out" the place to satisfy his curiosity.

He stayed after hours one night in the VIP lounge and felt a strange presence when he heard unexplainable noises including a "whooshing" sound, and witnessed doors opening, flashes of light, and moving bottles.

According to New Jersey psychic Jane Doherty, who has held séances at the nightspot, Liquid Assets is actually haunted by several spirits. She says Vincent "Mad Dog" Coll and brothers, "Bar Rags" and Jerry "Chin" Iadarola, (the deceased uncles of Liquid Assets' owner, John Colasanti) are the culprits.

Coll and the Iadarola brothers were partners-in-crime in the Bronx during the prohibition era.

Doherty identifies another spirit whose name may be "Ariel," a woman who died in a car accident on her way to work at the club several years ago.

Liquid Assets' security cameras filmed a diaphanous figure flitting about the bar's rear parking lot. A gossamer form darted up, down, and around whizzing in and out of camera range.

The alarm company that installed the system cannot explain the anomaly and the inexplicable image is only visible on the security screen - not by anyone outside. The strange form disappears when any person enters the lot - a deliveryman, police or patron, indicating some kind of reasoning ability.

Doherty thinks the mysterious image is the spirit of one of the bootleggers who ran the inn as a speakeasy. That would explain the entity's furtive behavior.

The phantom purveyor may feel he's inside the building because the bar is now one level opposed to its former days as a two-story inn that covered much of what is now the parking lot.

Not only does Doherty believe the spirit of the young woman, who was a dancer, inhabits the club, she says a young man's spirit frequents the joint because he enjoys the friendly atmosphere.

Some other ghostly antics include bar stools and glasses spontaneously moving and spigots fly out of their holders. Disembodied entities poke the help in the back (a spectral hold-up?) and gently tug at the female employees' long hair.

Some feel the paranormal activity is exaggerated here, but the security videotape remains an "unexplained occurrence."

The anomaly on the digital recording cannot be explained nor can it be reproduced. Light, smoke, birds, bats, and bugs have all been ruled out and the camera is not defective. The security company's spokesperson said the digital recording is timed and dated and impossible to alter.

Check out the videotapes from Liquid Assets' surveillance cameras yourself on their website: www.liquidassetsnj.com.

HISTORIC WALNFORD
Upper Freehold

Hidden away off Route 539 in Upper Freehold is Historic Walnford, the centerpiece of Monmouth County's 1098-acre Crosswicks Creek Park.

America's first industry was milling and in 1734 a village was founded on this site around a gristmill, much like nearby Allentown.

During the unsettled days before the Revolution, Richard Waln moved his family from Philadelphia to the seclusion of Upper Freehold. The international merchant-trader owned a wharf in Philadelphia, which gave him an advantage over competing mills in the area. Crosswicks Creek powered the mills and was used as a water highway for transporting goods from Walnford to market in Philadelphia.

With his son Nicholas at the helm as full time farmer and milling merchant, Walnford reached its peak of production in the early 19th century when 50 people lived and worked on the 1,300-acre estate.

When Nicholas died in 1848 his wife and daughter managed the homestead. Due to changes in milling and farming, by the close of the 19th century, daughter Sarah Waln Hendrickson, who was widowed at age 41, sadly realized Walnford's prosperity had seen better days. Business dwindled to milling corn and grain for area customers.

The specter of a woman in black has been spotted at historic Walnford.

Sarah's nephew acquired the estate after her death in 1907 and transformed the property into a pastoral weekend retreat.

Today the 250-year-old mill village includes a corn crib, an 1879 carriage house, cow barn, grist mill, and the 1773 Waln House, the home of a resident spirit.

Those who have noticed the shade describe the specter as a woman in black. When seen she is spotted at the top of the main staircase.

Another spooky anomaly is that some cupboard doors refuse to stay closed. While visiting with spirit photographers, we were discussing this oddity with our tour guide Sarah Bent, the site's supervisor. Quite boldly, the door on a cabinet over the stairs near the servants' quarters opened in front of our eyes. The action was deliberate, not the slow movement of an unbalanced door.

Phyllis Sabia quickly shot some photos and a huge orb appeared in one of the pictures. Downstairs in the kitchen, another one of her snapshots revealed a woman's face contained inside an orb.

On a previous visit, one of Theresa Roguskie's photographs captured a misty ectoplasm swirling in the nearby servant's quarters.

Ms. Bent gave us a rare peek of the attic where one of Theresa's photos revealed another orb.

Perhaps Sarah Waln Hendrickson is not the only spirit in the historic house...

The Walns occupied the property for 200 years. If Sara's spirit counts as tenancy, the family history here is well into its third century.

THE VERNON INN
Vernon

John Vandegriff built the Vernon Inn in 1833 and the tavern has been in business ever since. During the 19th and 20th centuries the tavern, located on Route 94 just north of Route 515, served the town as a principal gathering place for public meetings, assemblies, voting, and the like.

In 1936 the inn suffered a devastating fire when a squirrel knocked over a kerosene lamp in the attic. The conflagration resulted in one casualty and necessitated extensive rebuilding.

New owners purchased the property in 2003 and refurbished the structure that serves as a restaurant, tavern, and apartments.

Some individuals who live and work there say that occasionally televisions change channels by unknown means and lights go on and off. Sudden chills in an otherwise warm environment are commonplace. And then there are the night noises...

The liquor storage room in the basement is kept locked for obvious reasons. A bartender remarked that he sometimes finds the door violently rattling and shaking like there's someone on the other side trying desperately to get out. Could this be the desperate spirit of the unfortunate being trapped in the building during the fire?

Investigators from the North Jersey Paranormal Research group snapped photos in the cellar that revealed floating orbs, unseen to the naked eye. While inspecting the space they also heard a tremendous "bang" and were unable to determine the source.

Orb activity captured with digital cameras was prevalent in the rear dining area and on the stairs leading to the upstairs apartments. Videotape caught a streaking orb in the dining room as well.

The group utilized electromagnetic field detectors that reflected abnormally high readings, which could be indicative of an invisible presence.

One night after closing an employee, who was alone in a back storeroom, distinctly heard a male voice say "Good evening." The worker hot-tailed it out of there to seek the comfort and security of his associates on the other side of the building. Returning to the storage room to check out the incident, the group discovered the area was ice cold, *most* unusual because it was a summer night; since the space has no ventilation, the room is normally quite warm.

Employees notice lights turning on and off, doors opening and closing on their own, and obscure shapes traveling about the building.

Recently, the owner and a bartender watched a male apparition dressed in a full-length, teal colored coat walk across the dining area and vanish.[7] Ghost investigators' video showed a string of three orbs in the same area.

The paranormal group also recorded a child's voice calling out: "Hey!" and a few seconds later the words "quiet, quiet," followed by a soft sigh.

---

[7] www.nnjpr.org

BAHIA VISTA
West Atlantic City

The Spanish style castle that once rose from the sand dunes was called the "Barbara Hutton" mansion. A misnomer because five and dime store magnate F. W. Woolworth's granddaughter only visited occasionally.

Barbara Hutton's aunt Grace Hutton Middleton, custom-built "Bahia Vista" in 1926 long before the property offered spectacular casino views. In the opulent mansion's declining years the dilapidated building gained a dark reputation. Old-timers on the Atlantic City boardwalk swore the place was haunted.

What's intriguing about this particular site is that it's one of three Woolworth-related properties of eerie character. Bahia Vista bears certain similarities to *Winfield*, the Woolworth estate in Oyster Bay on Long Island, New York, a *very* haunted location as recounted in the author's *Haunted Long Island*.

According to Monica Randall, who wrote the book *Winfield*, a visitor inside Bahia Vista claimed there was a Latin inscription above a coat of arms that translated to "Regard the Demon." This same guest said there was a black mirror[8] set into a wall upstairs - just like it was at Woolworth's ghostly manse.

---

[8] Scrying is the ancient technique of gazing into an object such as a crystal ball for the purposes of divination. Some people achieve visions from gazing into flames, a shallow bowl of water, black ink, or a black mirror.

Some say that a stable boy and his inconsolable lover haunt Monmouth University's Lauren K. Woods theatre.

LAUREN K. WOODS THEATRE
West Long Branch

In *Ghosts of the Garden State II*, the Guggenheim Library on the campus of Monmouth University was presented as a haunted site. It appears that another university building, also once owned by the Guggenheims, qualifies as a spirited realm.

The Lauren K. Woods Theatre at Monmouth University used to be the carriage house for Murry and Leonie Guggenheim on their summer estate. Later transformed into the Guggenheim Theatre, the playhouse has its own haunted history.

The prevailing story is that a stable boy suffered an accidental death and his inconsolable lover committed suicide by hanging.

Staffers at the theater could not confirm the stories, but neighbors report apparitions of the young man, and some theatergoers hear the sound of someone weeping overhead.

HUDSON COUNTY COMMUNITY COLLEGE
West New York

Hudson County Community College provides educational services at a number of centers throughout the county, including the college's Bilingual Center in West New York housed in the former Our Lady Help of Christians convent. In view of that detail, it's no surprise that the resident wraith is a nun.

Security guards have had plenty of firsthand experiences with the ethereal nun. Several times one worker heard audible footsteps like someone walking behind him but when he turned around no one was there. Another watchman discerned indistinct voices.

The men say the sisterly spook manifests as a classic Mother Superior-type and her authoritative specter gives the distinct impression that "she doesn't want us here." On the contrary, other workers who sensed the holy ghost, claim she appears as a benevolent spirit. Perhaps there is more than one ethereal nun in residence.

One instructor reported seeing a nun's apparition. He observed a woman in a black dress walk out of the bathroom with an armful of books. When he followed her into his classroom, no one was there.

The Archdiocese of Newark owns the building along with Our Lady Help of Christians church and rectory. A spokesperson denied paranormal activity at these locations but another staffer suggested that the rectory is also haunted.

ACKNOWLEDGEMENTS

I want to thank my "ghost friends," Theresa Roguskie and Phyllis Sabia for their high-spirited camaraderie and for sharing their spectral snapshots.

I am also grateful to Susan Grahn for her continuing supply of ghostly material.

This book is possible thanks to the information offered by the Black Forest Restaurant's Chef Keith and his assistant Bill Van Pelt; Director Andrew Sandall of The Hermitage; Sarah Bent and Maggie Stroehlein, Historic Walnford; Tom Peterson at Hollyberries; Trish Hruska and Barbara Mocarski of Howell Township; Cookie Kaizer, Old Stone House Village; Donald J. Peck, Proprietary House; Patrick TeeVan, Publick House bartender; Jackie Widows, Raritan Public Library; and Erika Gorder and David A. D'Onofrio, Rutgers University Libraries.

"The reason we're so interested in hauntings
is because it shows life goes on - the soul survives."

Sylvia Brown

BIBLIOGRAPHY

Brienza, Mary. "Weird RU." *The Daily Targum*, 10/31/03.

Brown, Kimberly. " Getting Into The Spirit Of Things." *The Star Ledger*, October 31, 1998.

Chesek, Tom, "Ghosts In The House 'Turn of the Screw' at Monmouth U." *Asbury Park Press*, June 18, 2004.

Churpakovich, Patricia. "Local cemetery yields haunting tales of borough folklore." *Jersey Journal*; October 28, 2004.

Coscarelli, Kate. "A Haunting Concern." *The Star Ledger*; October 31, 1998.

Daye, Stephanie. "Jersey City bar has some regular customers that aren't so regular." *Jersey Journal*; October 30, 2004.

DiIonno, Mark. *A Guide to New Jersey's Revolutionary War Trail*. Rutgers University Press; 2000.

Ferrante, Valerie A. "Country Sisters." *Forked River Gazette*, May 2004.

Jaccarino, Mike. "Barnegat Shop Owner Recounts Odd Happenings." *The Press of Atlantic City*, October 30, 2004.

Landrum, Mahala, "The Sheriff's Daughter." *Forked River Gazette*, February 2004.

Miller, Michael. "Ghost hunters to investigate 'haunted' home." *Press of Atlantic City*, May 17, 2003.

Marhoefer, Laurie. "Ghost Stories at the Surflight Theater." *The Press of Atlantic City*, October 25, 2001.

Mays, Jeffery C. "History is embedded in every square foot of Belleville's Dutch Reformed Church. "*The Star Ledger*, September 5, 1999.

Monmouth County Park. *Historic Walnford* brochure.

Nevitt, Cindy. "Restaurants That Go Bump In The Night." *At the Shore*; October 30, 1998.

Ortloff, George C. *A Lady in the Lake*. With Pipe and

Book Publishers; 1985.

Pezzuto, Elizabeth Brown. "My Summer Vacations At The Batsto Mansion." www.members/tripod.com.

Pritchard, Michael. "Ghost Stories, If You Believe." *The Press of Atlantic City*, October 26, 2003.

Quirk, James. "Our House Is An Old Haunt For 18th Century Spirits." *Asbury Park Press*, June 6, 2000.

Randall, Monica. *Winfield*. St. Martin's Press; 2003.

Rose, Lisa. "Ghosts aside, tavern is a pleasant haunt." *The Star Ledger*, April 25, 2003.

Ruderman, Wendy. "This one's a scream." *Philadelphia Inquirer*, November 28, 2004.

Schmidt, George P. *Douglass College: A History*. Rutgers University Press; 1968.

Schneider, Kate. "Reporter's Notebook." www.straussnews.com, October 27, 2004.

Underdue, Towanda. "Close encounters of the haunted kind. *The Star Ledger*, June 13, 2002.

Young, Elise. "Ghost stories." *NJMonthly*; February 2003.

Websites

Allentown: www.allentown.nj.com

Batsto Village: www.batstovillage.org

Hereford Inlet Lighthouse: wwwherefordlighthouse.org

The Hermitage: www.hermitage.org

Lost in New Jersey: www.lostinnewjersey.com

The Midnight Society: www.midnightsociety.com

North Jersey Paranormal Research: www.nnjpr.org

Our House Restaurant: www.ourhouserestaurant.net

Raritan Library: www.raritanlibrary.org

South Jersey Paranormal Research: www.sjpr.org

Sunnybank: www.sunnybankcollies.us

Surflight Theater: www.surflight.org

Tennent Church: www.oldtennentchurch.org

Tri-State Paranormal Research: www.tsprghosts.com

Union County: www.unioncounty.org

BLACK CAT PRESS...
Post Office Box 1218, Forked River, New Jersey 08731
E-mail: llmacken@hotmail.com

...Publishes **13** <u>Scary</u> titles by
Lynda Lee Macken!

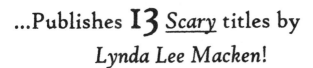

ADIRONDACK GHOSTS
Haunted Places in New York's North Country
ISBN 0-9700718-1-7 ~ $7.95

ADIRONDACK GHOSTS II
More Haunted Places in New York's North Country
ISBN 0-9700718-6-8 ~ $8.95

EMPIRE GHOSTS
New York State's Haunted Landmarks
ISBN 0-9700718-8-4 ~ $8.95

LEATHERSTOCKING GHOSTS
Haunted Places in Central New York
ISBN 0-9755244-2-9 ~ $8.95

HAUNTED LONG ISLAND
Ghosts & Haunted Places in New York's
Nassau & Suffolk Counties
ISBN 0-9755244-0-2 ~ $8.95

GHOSTLY GOTHAM
New York City's Haunted History
ISBN 0-9700718-4-1 ~ $9.95

HAUNTED HISTORY OF STATEN ISLAND
Mysterious People & Places in
New York's Richmond County
ISBN 0-9700718-0-9 ~ $7.95

GHOSTS OF THE GARDEN STATE
Haunted Places in New Jersey
ISBN 0-9700718-2-5~ $7.95

GHOSTS OF THE GARDEN STATE II
ISBN 0-9700718-7-6 ~ $8.95

GHOSTS OF THE GARDEN STATE III
More Haunted Places in New Jersey
ISBN 0-9755244-1-0 ~ $8.95

HAUNTED CAPE MAY
ISBN 0-9700718-5-X ~ $8.95

HAUNTED SALEM & BEYOND
Witchcraft, Commerce, Seafarers & Slaves
ISBN 0-9700718-3-3 ~ $7.95

HAUNTED BALTIMORE
Charm City's Spirits
ISBN 0-9700718-9-2 ~ $8.95

All books available at most bookstores and on-line,
or send $1.50 postage for <u>each</u> title ordered to:

BLACK CAT PRESS
Post Office Box 1218
Forked River, New Jersey 08731